A Journey Through Corporate Challenges: Exploring The Art Of Following The Process

Yolanda Narain

ACKNOWLEDGEMENTS

I am deeply grateful to my family, friends, and colleagues for their unwavering support and understanding throughout this incredible literary journey. Your constant encouragement and belief in this work have been an endless source of inspiration. A special shout-out to my dear friend Ana Maria Mayo, who has been there for me since my younger days of doubt and fear. I would also like to thank my colleague and friend, Ines Silva. During one of our countless interactions at work, she astutely observed, "You have a wealth of captivating stories to tell. Your storytelling skills are truly remarkable." This simple yet generous statement marked the beginning of an incredible journey.

And to you, the reader, I am deeply grateful for your time and commitment to understanding my experiences. I hope your interest in my professional journey will broaden, deepen, and enrich your own.

DEDICATION

This book is dedicated to you, the reader, who is driven by common sense rather than fear!

TABLE OF CONTENTS

CHAPTER 1

INTRODUCTION

E ver since my childhood, I've been driven by an insatiable curiosity. Questions like "How did the world begin?" "Why is the sun yellow?" "How big is the universe?" and even the more mundane "Why do I have to eat vegetables?" were constantly on my mind. My parents had an easy answer for that last one. Because.

Not everything captured my interest, but once something did, it consumed me. I remember losing myself for hours, staring out the window, deep in thought, trying to unravel the sequence of events that my young eyes deemed crucial. I would dissect each component, breaking it down until almost nothing was left.

Then came the exciting part—reconstruction. I would put the pieces back together to create something new. Sometimes, the results were straightforward, and only when I was satisfied with my creation would I move on to other pursuits.

I was intrigued by how individual pieces moved, interacted, and influenced each other. Over time, I became adept at predicting where things were coming from or where they were going as vivid patterns danced in my mind. It felt like magic. I grasped the concepts of *expectation, predictability*, and *simplification*, even if those terms hadn't yet entered my vocabulary. I learned to anticipate events and forecast outcomes.

Why did everything seem so complex when it should have been simple? I often felt frustrated by my inability to understand. Little did I know that my curiosity and desire to make sense of the world would shape my future career.

People, too, fascinated me with their unpredictability. I wondered why they behaved in specific ways and sometimes tried to guess their reactions. This was often disheartening, as I was frequently wrong. I learned that with people, it's best to "prepare for the best but expect the worst."

Choosing a university major was a monumental decision. Torn between psychology and the biological sciences, I finally settled on the latter, drawn to understanding living systems from cells to ecosystems. I didn't realise then that these systems mirror the structure of corporations—essentially collections of cells in the form of people.

My fascination with processes and people converged when I started working at a pharmaceutical company over twenty years ago. My tendency to overthink and question issues, which I often found annoying, began to pay off. Anticipating events gave me an edge, though it was not immediately appreciated. I usually felt out of place and misunderstood.

Those were tough times, and it took years to find the missing link. I could see beyond the immediate issue but struggled to communicate my insights. Once I understood this, everything changed. My focus shifted to "how"—how to help others see what I saw. It was no longer about me; it was about them or, better still, *us*.

This book recounts the events, observations, and memorable moments from my years in business. In retrospect, many of these events are humorous, though they didn't seem so then. Distance and time allow us to look back and laugh at our mistakes—and even ourselves.

CHAPTER 2

IT CANNOT BE THIS SIMPLE, CAN IT?

In this chapter, I will explore the narrative of a project team's journey through an unforeseen challenge within the business process under their purview. By the chapter's conclusion, you will find a distillation of the events and lessons from this experience. My role in this narrative is crucial since it is through my experiences and insights that I began to understand the complexities of managing global business processes.

Several years ago, I embarked on a new professional chapter by joining an international company based in Europe. My inaugural task within this organisation was to take ownership of a global business process that had operated for several years post-implementation. This responsibility encompassed full accountability for the process's daily operations, strategic direction, standardisation efforts, quality and compliance measures, procedural documentation, and training initiatives.

The process in question had been meticulously designed and successfully rolled out a few years before I arrived in response to the emergence of a new regulatory requirement. It was a critical component of the company's operations, ensuring alignment with legal standards while optimising efficiency and effectiveness across various business units.

As the new custodian of this process, I was tasked with maintaining its integrity, identifying opportunities for enhancement, and ensuring its continued compliance with evolving regulatory landscapes. The challenges faced by the project team and the strategies employed to overcome them form the crux of this chapter, offering insights into the complexities of managing global business processes in a dynamic and regulated environment.

Ready, Steady, Go

In the face of the new regulations released by the authorities, the company undertook a comprehensive impact assessment across all its business processes. The findings revealed that several methods, including the one I was responsible for, required updates to comply with the new requirements. This process had been under scrutiny by regulators across the industry, highlighting the critical nature of the updates. The company's commitment to compliance was unwavering, instilling confidence in the business's operations.

The process was not overly complex, resembling a decision tree with a straightforward initial question: "Which document should we use to manage this process, A or B?" This question was posed to the process end-users and relied on operational information shared across different functions and systems. Gathering this data was both time-consuming and resource-intensive. Despite occasional errors and deviations, the process appeared to be functioning well. However, updates to other processes led the project team to assume that the necessary operational information would continue to be provided.

This assumption taught me a critical lesson: *"Be cautious with your assumptions."* I will elaborate on this point later in the book.

Three weeks before the *"go-live"* date, we discovered that decisions made elsewhere affected our process.

At a meeting organised by others to discuss data gathering for their new process, it became evident that the information we needed would not be provided in the required format. A participant's comment, *"We have discussed this topic many times; why are we discussing it again?"* caught me off guard. It highlighted a crucial distinction: *discussions* and *decisions* are two separate things.

Discussions involve colleagues sharing and exchanging ideas and views without consensus or conclusion. Conversely, decisions require a conclusion reached through agreement or compromise, often involving a choice and an execution plan.

Confusion between discussions and decisions is expected. Teams may be stuck in endless discussions about the same topic, never progressing. The question, *"Why are we discussing this again?"* often indicates no decision has been made. A leader's role is to foster an environment where good discussions lead to sound decisions, a responsibility frequently overlooked.

Another example. The same topic was discussed for the third time that week in one project meeting. I was new to the project but recognised the team's uncertainty and the mounting pressure of the timelines. I intervened before the meeting ended, suggesting a decision be made that day. The team agreed, and despite some disappointment with the outcome, we had a direction.

This experience taught me that indecision can be worse than making the wrong decision. Indecision can lead to missed opportunities and increased stress, while a wrong decision can provide valuable feedback and new opportunities.

Documenting decisions is equally important. As I learned in compliance, "If it's not documented, it didn't happen." I made it a practice to promptly produce and distribute meeting minutes after each meeting, requesting feedback and updating them accordingly. This documentation ensured that everyone was aligned and moving forward.

The events and lessons from this experience underscore the importance of *transparent decision-making*, the *distinction between discussions and decisions*, and *the critical role of documentation in ensuring a project's success*.

Back to the main story

A critical issue occurred in the business process just three weeks before the go-live date, propelling us into crisis mode. An emergency meeting was convened for that day.

As I broke the unexpected news, the team was visibly shocked. Their reactions were a mix of disbelief and immediate discussion, but I'll spare the details here. Years have passed since that meeting, and although we were all frustrated then, I can't help but smile when I reflect on those moments, armed with the knowledge I now have: it was just the beginning of my corporate education.

I had no idea then that this unforeseen trouble would lead to one of the most significant and impactful process simplifications I've ever participated in.

A hidden gift

The atmosphere in the meeting was sombre as we grappled with our frustration and disappointment. Yet, we were acutely aware of the need for swift action. Time was of the essence, and the situation demanded immediate attention. If there was one, the silver lining was that we were dealing with a well-defined problem with clear objectives and potential solutions.

I initiated the discussion with a straightforward, assertive question: *"What do we do now?"* Ideas began to emerge. Initially, the project team considered two main options:

1. Revert to the previous process: This would entail returning to the old way of doing things despite the cumbersome and intricate nature of the information-gathering process. This option would also set back other processes.

2. Create a new process: This approach would ensure access to the necessary information. However, the existing decision tree was already complex, and introducing another layer would only compound the complexity and inefficiency.

Reflecting on a recent corporate communication that underscored the importance of simplifying all business processes, I was struck by a recurring thought: *"So much energy is expended on simplifying processes rather than creating and managing simple ones from the outset. If we started with simple processes and managed them effectively, simplification would not be needed later."*

It's even more intriguing to note that the very colleagues now advocating for simplification were often the same people who had a hand in creating or perpetuating the complex processes in the first place. One could argue that they were perhaps new to the environment or lacked the experience and foresight to avoid complexity.

This reminds me once when a senior colleague asked, *"Why are we making this so complicated? We need to simplify it."* A meeting was promptly scheduled, and my calendar, along with that of 14+ other participants, was updated accordingly. I couldn't help but think, *"Really?"*

While there was a certain logic to pursuing one of the proposed options, doing so would have meant overlooking the magical opportunity.

The beauty of data

I previously mentioned that the crux of this process revolved around a decision tree, which involved choosing between Document A and Document B in a specific context at a given time.

Given that the process had been effectively running in the company for years, I was curious about the frequency and conditions under which each document was selected. The project team agreed that Document A was the more commonly chosen option, but we hadn't explored it further. Our first step was to analyse in-house data to get the exact numbers; this became our top priority.

Soon after the meeting, the data was in front of us. Over five years, the selection had occurred 500 times, with Document A chosen 475 times and Document B only 25 times. This disparity was unexpected, and we felt optimistic about leveraging this insight. The team questioned why a complex process was in place to accommodate a 5% exception rate and sought to understand its rationale.

You might think we strayed from our initial challenge of securing the operational information we needed, and you'd be right. However, the team's investigation went beyond the initial question.

As we scrutinised the data, we hoped to identify a pattern or trend that would allow us to handle the exceptions separately from the primary process and decision tree. *"If those 5% were of the same type or category, we could manage them differently,"* we thought. But our hopes were dashed when further data revealed that the exceptions couldn't be grouped under any single concept or scenario. The new process diagram I had envisioned crumbled. Then, I remembered a pivotal moment.

Months earlier, during a project meeting, a participant had posed a challenging question that had been on his mind for some time. We had discussed this topic before, and his question still resonates: *"Why are we selecting Document B? The regulations don't specify this; we don't need to do it."*

I didn't fully grasp his point then, as I was still gripping the project's intricacies. I acknowledged his concerns but assumed there was a valid reason for the current approach—an easy way out for me.

As I recalled his question, everything clicked. I immediately went back to him to revisit our earlier conversation. *"Are you saying we could have chosen Document A in those 5% of cases, too?"* I asked. *"I don't see why not,"* he responded.

This brings us to a crucial concept: *assumptions.*

We accept assumptions as accurate without proof, often unaware we're making them. Assumptions are easier than facts because they require less effort—no need for questioning or thinking. In a decision meeting, if information is missing from another department, it's easier to assume than to reach out and validate. These assumptions can become the basis for decisions, leading to reactive scrambles when found to be incorrect.

In our case, I assumed there was a good reason for the existing process, and there was. However, I failed to consider alternatives, efficiency, or the appropriateness of options in a dynamic business environment.

The role of assumptions in communication is equally fascinating. When we communicate, we assume the audience understands by default. How often do presenters check for understanding beyond a cursory *"Any questions?"*

We also blame the audience for misunderstandings, assuming their fault is not ours. A later chapter explores effective communication and the pitfalls of assumptions in depth.

Get the correct answer, and ask the right question

The response from my colleague, *"I don't see why not,"* was intriguing not only because it suggested there was no apparent reason not to adopt a new approach but also because it indicated a shift in our investigative approach. Instead of proving the new approach was appropriate, we focused on identifying why it couldn't be.

This was an unusual and exciting activity that engaged everyone. We were looking for reasons not to change, knowing that team members would invest time and energy searching for potential issues rather than benefits. The human brain loves habits, resists change, and is wired to conserve energy, prioritizing negative information over positive—a phenomenon I've never fully understood but is fundamentally true.

Our question was, *"If we were to choose Document A with no option for Document B, is there any risk of non-compliance?"* Despite consulting regulations, regulator blogs, and other communications, we couldn't find a clear answer, which was good news, though hard to believe for some.

In hindsight, this shouldn't have been surprising. Regulations typically cover common scenarios, often overlooking exceptional cases. In such situations, we make assumptions or inferences based on the norm.

Further discussions with experts revealed a fascinating insight: not only would choosing Document A over Document B not pose a compliance risk, but it would also align with a more robust and conservative regulatory approach.

The project team was both excited and sceptical. There was no evidence to suggest that selecting Document A would be inappropriate for those rare cases.

A Short Detour

Stakeholders

Process stakeholders are individuals or groups that either carry out the process, impact its performance, or are affected by its outcome, whether positively or negatively. Identifying stakeholders early and understanding how your actions affect them is crucial for the long-term success and viability of new processes. Any new project should begin with a stakeholder analysis. Stakeholders are classified based on their influence, interest, or involvement in the project, typically falling into three categories:

Primary stakeholders are directly affected by the process, either positively or negatively. Process end-users who use or follow a business process as part of their work are in this category.

Secondary stakeholders are indirectly affected by the business process. This group includes those whose professions or jobs might be influenced by the process.

Key stakeholders are critical figures involved in or influencing the planning, execution, or outcome of a business process. They can also belong to either of the other two categories mentioned above.

Back to the story

The project team considered altering the status quo, necessitating engagement with those involved in the initial design. Some were still with the company and offered valuable insights and recommendations for the new approach.

We contacted affiliates and other experts in the field, ensuring no one was left out. I recall some of their reactions as they became acquainted with the topic: *"Oh, finally..."*, *"Absolutely, that's not a problem,"* *"Oh wow, that makes complete sense because..."*

What did this mean for the process and the decision tree described at the story's beginning? With the new method, the starting question could be answered without the operational information from other functions; this information was no longer necessary.

Reflecting on those days, I'm reminded of a quote by Albert Einstein: *"If I had an hour to solve a problem, I'd spend 55 minutes thinking* about the problem and five minutes thinking about solutions.*"* Einstein's quote is more than just an intriguing remark by one of the most brilliant people in history; it encapsulates a fundamental truth about problem-solving that is often overlooked. It emphasizes the importance of deeply understanding a problem before attempting to solve it. This is what we did, this time without assumptions or inferences.

Long before the end of our investigation, I had a hunch about the path we were about to take. With a mix of excitement and fear, I sought management's support. I was terrified, experiencing the primal "fear of change" in anticipation of what would come.

This brings me to another concept: *questioning.*

Asking *"WHY"* multiple times can lead you beyond the obvious to uncover the root cause of any problem or concern. I've known this since I was young, challenging my parents daily with my inquisitiveness! What I now understand as *"root cause analysis"* was then the equivalent of continuously asking *"why"* until exhaustion. For instance, I wondered why, as a child, I had to go to bed early. After the second or third *"why,"* I'd get the same answer: *"Because I said so."* With that response, I knew there was no point in asking further, and I'd throw a tantrum on my way to the bedroom.

In a corporate setting, asking colleagues *"WHY"* is a simple and effective way to understand why specific tasks are performed in a particular way. This technique can produce excellent results, especially when the answer is, *"Because that's how we've always done it."* This response is typical, and I always feel excited when I hear it: *"Great, so now we can change it then!"* I always think.

This could not be this simple, could it?

The team acknowledged and accepted that the three-week deadline would not be met. However, this wasn't a significant issue, as organizations have mechanisms and tools to manage such situations. A planned process deviation was put in place, giving us time to think, decide, and execute.

After four weeks of thorough investigation, we felt we had gone back far enough in our search for impediments or concerns. No matter how hard we tried, we couldn't find a reason why we couldn't take the project in a different direction. The more we investigated, the stronger our case became.

The new process decision started with the question: "Which document should we use to manage this process, A or B?" However, the response differed: "Select Document A if available. If not available, use Document B."

The new approach transformed the process landscape. The simplicity of the selection tree surprised everyone on the team and the end users, who were all too familiar with the vast amounts of time and resources they had invested. I remember one team member asking in disbelief, *"But it can't be this simple, can it?"* To which I replied, *"It can, and it is!"*

This is an incredible case of process simplification—not just because of the simplification itself and it impacts on the organisation (e.g., reducing required resources) but because of how it all unfolded.

At this point, there are two concepts here that I'd like to highlight: *complexity and simplicity.*

The Cambridge Dictionary defines complexity as *"the state of having many parts and being difficult to understand or find an answer to"* and simplicity as *"the fact that something is easy to understand or do."* Simplification means making something less complex, complicated, plainer, or more straightforward. Most of you have likely heard the phrase *"keep it simple"* and would agree with statements like *"less is more."* So why do we insist on making everything so complicated?

Complexity is a natural side effect of growth; as your business grows, it will encounter complexity. That's why clarifying, reducing complexity, and adapting to it is crucial. This is where organizational agility comes into play.

When focusing on business processes, simplification allows us to challenge each process and approach to identify the most efficient and best-suited one for a particular purpose. We ask what is causing complexity, how everything is connected, and what the most essential pieces of the process are.

However, why do processes become complex over time? This may be due to the cumulative by-product of organizational changes. While this may be true, it still doesn't answer the question. Why would changes result in a complex process over time? Moreover, were those changes indeed required or necessary?

This is where the concept of *"complexity bias"* comes into play. It's one of the most common biases discussed by social psychologists and describes the human tendency to prefer complicated explanations and solutions over simple ones. This tendency leads to two things: first, it makes us think that complex solutions are better than simple ones because they are complicated. Second, it makes us afraid of simple explanations for fear that they might be too obvious or not comprehensive enough.

We may not realise it, but complexity bias can lead us astray in many ways, from choosing a face cream to selecting a new restaurant for dinner.

A Short Detour

Here, I'd like to mention the use of *jargon*. Jargon is a specific word or expression used by a particular profession or group that is generally difficult for others to understand. Many consider jargon unnecessarily complicated language used to impress rather than inform the audience. Complexity bias could explain why jargon is popular among academics, politicians, business leaders, or anyone wanting to feel important. We might ignore or dismiss simple explanations for fear that they might make us sound unintelligent.

I've observed a similar tendency in the business environment when decisions are made. Decision-makers are likelier to choose an option that seems more complex, even when more straightforward options are available. The more convoluted or complex something seems, the more likely people will be attracted to it. However, what Occam's razor philosophical principle advises during decision-making is the opposite. The English Franciscan friar and philosopher William of Ockham suggests that all else being equal, the simplest explanation or solution with the fewest assumptions is most likely the correct one.

Nonetheless, complexity bias does bring some benefits. In terms of creativity (e.g., brainstorming exercises), adding complexity allows for flexibility in thinking and encourages group members to think outside the box.

Back to the story

Only one thing remained for the team to do: *make a formal decision.*

The fear room

I informed the team that a formal final decision was needed, and a meeting was scheduled for this purpose, with all team members required to attend. I vividly remember that meeting as if it were yesterday; how could I forget?

The meeting began with a presentation of the research and information gathered over the previous weeks, including regulations, in-house data, stakeholder feedback, and historical aspects of the process. We discussed the data and addressed any questions raised by the participants. Then, the pivotal question: "Shall we change the current process and adopt the new approach?"

There was a moment of silence. Despite the data fully supporting and encouraging the *"go ahead"* for the new alternative, an overwhelming silence lingered; no one spoke. I emphasised the need for a formal decision based on the presented data and that any concerns or additional considerations could still be raised. I asked the question again but still met with silence. Regardless of the data favouring the new approach, the team hesitated to make this decision, but I understood why: the fear of change. However, I want to reassure you all that we are here to support you every step of the way.

I adopted a different strategy: *"Is there any reason, problem, or concern as to why we couldn't change to the new approach?"*

This question seemed more approachable for the team, and one by one, they confirmed they saw no reason to prevent the implementation of the new option. Some responded, *"As of today, I see no reason..."* This collective understanding and agreement from the team was a testament to their knowledge and expertise, and I realized this was as close to a decision as I would get, and it was enough for me. That was it; we had a formal decision.

Overcoming the Fear of Change

Fear of change often stems from our experiences and natural tendency to stick to familiar things. Our brains favour routine and predictability, creating a sense of safety.

Change is an inevitable part of working life, and managing change effectively for an organization and a team has become a core competency for managers or leaders. For many, change brings uncertainty, anxiety, and stress. Some reasons people fear change in the work environment include:

- Lack of awareness about the reason for the change: confusion. People may fear change if they don't understand why it's happening. For positive engagement, people need to know why the change is necessary. Additionally, as much as we might complain about our daily routines, they make us feel secure. A change in our routine, based on what we're familiar with, causes uncertainty, pushing people out of their comfort zones.

- Fear of lack of competence: People fear change if they doubt their ability to perform new tasks as expected. However, it's important to remember that our team is highly adaptable and capable. They might be afraid of appearing incompetent, and instead of sharing their concerns with their managers, they might prefer to disagree with the new approach or challenge the reason for the change.

- Additional work: People fear change because it might mean more work, and they might be right! Implementing change takes time and resources, while the business is expected to continue as usual. Struggles with workloads and lack of time can make people feel it's not worth the effort, preferring not to change.

- Exclusion from change-related decisions: losing control. People fear change because it might involve losing control over their

22

roles. No one likes feeling powerless. If the change is significant, people might feel it's being done to them.

In our story, changing the status quo likely triggered fear in most of the team.

The butterfly effect

The impact of process simplification on the organization, its people, and its processes was more significant than any of us could have anticipated. Implementing a streamlined and straightforward process decreased the likelihood of end-user errors and, therefore, increased regulatory compliance. The overall resource requirements in process management, including deviation management, were also reduced. I know no process deviations have been reported since the new process was implemented.

The team created new procedural documents that were half the length of the original ones, and one became redundant. End-user in-depth training was no longer required. However, the story doesn't end here. We received positive feedback from other functional groups, which still puzzles me today. When I thought I knew this process well, I didn't! I only knew what I could see, but the ramifications were much more profound than I had initially anticipated.

The butterfly effect, which also applies in the corporate environment, describes how small actions or decisions can have significant and far-reaching consequences. It's like a ripple in a pond—a tiny pebble can create a wave that reaches the shore. This effect often goes unnoticed, underscoring the importance of attention to detail and careful decision-making in our work.

Connecting the dots

The Cambridge Dictionary defines connecting the dots as "understanding the relationships between different facts or events." It's a metaphor frequently used to link disparate information or data points to understand a situation or problem better. For example, information from different sources can connect to form an unusual but beneficial concept.

This concept is widely used in business and large corporations. In this setting, multi-layered hierarchies and cross-functional teams are the operational models followed by most; the flow of information is multidirectional. Effective organization requires strong connections across different departments and access to information that may seem unrelated. These connections are not simple, which is why connecting the dots has become one of the most valuable skills to have in business. Dot connectors can see beyond the obvious.

These individuals can see the big picture and identify patterns and relationships between what may seem like unrelated ideas. It allows them to identify the root causes of problems and develop simple, innovative solutions very effectively. They are incredibly creative people with a sharp analytical mind that enables them to navigate challenges efficiently. Add practical communication skills, and you have your company's dream professional.

I recall once starting a new project for a new company. The first few meetings with the project team were intense, and the topics discussed seemed complex to me at the time. From the first moment, I noticed a general sense of frustration and some degree of confusion, too. As I explored the different aspects of the process, I had nothing else but questions. Some team members could answer many of them, but others remained unanswered: *"Oh, you don't want to go there"* or *"That's another can of worms"* are common answers. The *"can of worms"* pops up whenever trouble is anticipated. The same thought comes to mind: *"Why don't you open it and kill off the worms once and for all?"*

It seemed that aspects of the process were not addressed adequately and were not working as expected. *"These are too many issues; a connection between them must exist,"* I thought. It was like looking at the sky on a starry night but unable to see the constellations.

One very ordinary day, something came up. This seemed to be an essential concern for the team, and we decided to treat this as a priority. After exciting and animated discussions, we agreed on how to address the problem; everybody seemed pleased with the approach adopted and solved the problem. What we didn't expect was that, by addressing this particular concern, many other issues would automatically be resolved, too!

As I suspected, there was a connection between all the issues—a connection I can see now. Some of the more minor problems were downstream effects of the more significant upstream issue.

Summary and Lessons

What follows is a condensed version of the above story's sequence of events:

1. An unforeseen challenge arises.

2. Two potential solutions are identified but not immediately pursued.

3. A curious team member poses a simple question during a meeting.

4. The question is thoroughly researched and answered.

5. The team hits a roadblock.

6. A question asked half a year prior resurfaces as pertinent.

7. The team dives deeper into the issue, revisiting the initial problem.

8. A third option emerges as a viable solution.

9. The team reaches a decision.

10. A streamlined process is introduced.

In retrospect, the team could have opted for a quicker resolution by choosing between the initial two solutions or escalating the issue to senior management. However, a third option materialized seemingly out of nowhere by dedicating time to thoughtful consideration rather than hasty reactions and remaining open to alternatives. This journey was punctuated by two brief but transformative moments: a question sparked by curiosity and the recall of a past discussion.

Lessons from this story:

- Embrace Challenges as Opportunities: When confronted with an unexpected challenge, the team conducted a thorough assessment, discovering an opportunity that was promptly seized. This experience underscores the importance of examining challenges from multiple angles to uncover hidden opportunities.

- Return to Fundamentals: Instead of rushing to a solution, the team took a step back to retrace their steps and understand the root cause of the issue. This approach highlights the value of revisiting basics when progress seems elusive, as it can reveal alternative paths forward.

- Ask WHY: The team's repeated questioning of "why" led to a deeper comprehension of the process, illustrating how persistent inquiry can unravel complexity and enhance understanding.

- Leverage Data: Data were crucial in bolstering the team's arguments, making them more persuasive. This lesson emphasizes the power of data in supporting claims and driving decision-making.

- Re-examine Regulations: Approaching regulatory texts with fresh questions unveiled new insights that had previously gone unnoticed. This experience teaches the importance of revisiting regulations with a different perspective to discover new facets of a problem.

- Challenge Assumptions: The team learned not to take long-standing practices as the only or best way to perform tasks. This lesson highlights the importance of questioning assumptions and being open to alternative methods.

- Take your stakeholders with you: Building and nurturing relationships with stakeholders ensures trust and openness when discussing alternatives or challenges. This experience underscores the critical role of stakeholder management in fostering a collaborative environment.

- Acknowledge Fear in Change: The team recognized that fear is an inherent part of change but embraced the opportunity to streamline processes and enhance efficiency. This lesson teaches the importance of accepting fear as a natural response to change and not letting it hinder progress.

CHAPTER 3

A DREAM OUTCOME

This chapter will detail the intriguing events and situations I observed while working on specific business processes and teams. The main story in this section concerns a business process designed and implemented years before I joined the team. This process was not created in response to an inspection finding but was strongly associated with one.

Regulations require companies to perform certain activities periodically. However, they do not provide detailed instructions. The team designed the process as follows: Function A initiates the process; the workflow continues to Function B, then returns to Function A. Function A performs most activities, whereas Function B provides input into the process at an intermediate stage. The team agreed that these tasks would be performed annually and accepted that delays might occur under certain conditions. Different product teams performed the same activities at various times, resulting in a certain level of duplication.

What I know of those early days is that the team worked under extreme pressure with rigorous timelines. Limited expertise and no in-house data were available to assist decision-making. However, despite the challenges faced by the project team, they implemented a fully compliant process; the company adhered to the regulations.

Regulatory inspections

Many of you are probably familiar with regulatory inspections. The primary purpose of a regulatory inspection is to ensure that businesses comply with legal and ethical standards. These inspections are usually costly and time-consuming, requiring firms to dedicate significant resources to prepare and undergo the inspection.

This is possibly one of the most stressful parts of doing business for the company being examined. Uneasiness and stress arise when an inspector's visit is announced. Once the inspection ends, the outcome and results are summarized and communicated to all parties. One feels highly fortunate if no "critical finding" is reported, and the company welcomes the news with a profound sense of relief. However, when critical or significant findings are identified, the story changes. Disappointment and frustration settle in, and questions such as "How could this happen?" or "Who is accountable for the failure?" take precedence. Companies are set in motion to address the findings, and focused, dedicated teams are quickly assembled. As a starting point, they devise a plan and timelines for correcting and preventing errors. Negotiations with regulators and endorsements come next, and finally, the company executes the plan.

In a business setting, regulators are the primary stakeholders to appease, prioritizing implementing compliant business processes. However, another category of stakeholders, often neglected, is process end-users. *What is the point of having a process compliant with regulations (on paper) but not followed by the end user as intended?*

There is also the problem of tight timelines. In a reactive mode, time becomes a luxury that teams do not generally have. Under these conditions, highly structured meetings, clearly defined roles and responsibilities, and a practical decision-making process are crucial to project success.

Some weeks after joining this company, I was appointed the business process lead. In this new role, accountability for the maintenance, continuous improvement, and daily management of interlinked activities, as well as quality and compliance, remained with me.

Mind the gap

Even though the process itself was fully compliant, some deviations were reported over time. With each deviation, the team agreed upon and carefully executed corrective and preventive actions (CAPAs). CAPAs are the mechanism many companies use to fix problems and optimize processes. Adequate checks were also established to ensure that the preventive actions were effective and acceptable.

Gap analysis is a valuable tool for the initial assessment of a problem or situation. It's a structured way to identify the problem and support the search for solutions. This methodology seems designed to ask *"why"* continuously. It's possible that, without knowing, I constantly performed gap analysis during my childhood, although slightly more erratic and emotional.

A Short Detour

In this context, you may have heard of *"The five whys"* technique (or seven, depending on the experts). This technique involves asking *"why"* five times to determine the root cause of a problem or failure. I'm unsure how the experts determined these numbers; it depends on the problem or issue. In some circumstances, one answer may be enough; in other instances, you may need to ask *"why"* many more times, given that errors are often multi-faceted.

There's also another aspect to consider. When facing the same recurrent problem in a business process, the question might no longer be, *"Why is this happening?"* but *"Why is this happening often?"* This change of direction requires a deeper level of questioning, which often reveals a more significant or broader problem. Ultimately, the situation might require an innovative approach to get the process back on track.

Back to the story

Process deviations continued, and the preventive measures implemented did not work, as demonstrated by the effectiveness checks. This process relied on many different people and departments, each with its priorities and goals to achieve. *"In this setting, things can easily fall through the cracks,"* I often thought.

The process appeared well-documented, clearly describing roles, responsibilities, and activities. So why were there so many errors? Human errors happen regardless of how solid a process may be, but the unusually high number indicates something else. I began to question the business process as a whole; it seemed that the process itself was not working.

A Short Detour

The process ends with the user.

In general, the end-user is the person the process has been designed for. Because of this, their early involvement is critical. However, compliance is often the main driver of change in a regulated environment, and end-users are frequently overlooked. Regardless of the regulatory climate, early end-user engagement is essential because it determines the success of the business process. Although their early engagement may pose a challenge, especially when delivery timelines are tight, this does not have to be the case. Many strategies that do not require much investment can be highly appreciated by end-users: communication (presentations, emails, blogs, etc.), focused training, live demos, etc. Once the process goes live, their feedback provides valuable insights to determine if enhancements are required.

<u>Back to the story</u>

Several questions came to mind: Is the process robust enough? Are procedural documents written with the right level of detail? Is the process aligned with the end user's day-to-day activities? Do end-users have enough time to perform the activities described?

The team implemented corrective and preventive measures for each new error identified, but they kept coming. It was clear to everyone that these issues had to be managed differently; it was time to go back to the start and recheck the regulations. Does this sound familiar?

Discussions took place within the team, and other stakeholders got involved. Coincidentally, the quality department notified the team that an internal process audit would occur a few weeks later. Their investigations revealed several deficiencies we knew about and others we somehow suspected. This information was beneficial, as it clarified the actions the team had to take to get the process back on track. The team suspected this was not just an error-fixing exercise but required a much broader or deeper change.

Then, there was an email.

An ordinary email

On an ordinary day, I reviewed compliance data that had become available to the team. You might recall earlier when I described that certain activities were performed annually or sometimes longer, depending on specific circumstances. One day, something unusual caught my attention while reviewing quality data. There was one substantial delay in the performance of the activities in question. Function A was accountable for this part of the process, so I sent a query to them by email. I also CC'd other team members who I thought would want a follow-up on the issue. He confirmed that this was a standard scenario and that the company still complied with the regulations. He documented the rationale and relevant information for the team, and I closed the topic.

However, shortly after, Function B responded unexpectedly: *"We cannot afford to spend a long time without performing these activities; we are taking a big risk here!"* We all knew the process aligned with the regulations, so I suspected she was referring to something else. The bottom line was that Function B had difficulty accepting specific timelines, whereas Function A did not.

As already described, the business process was designed to meet a regulatory requirement for which Functions A and B were fully accountable. My colleague's response got me thinking, *"Is it possible that this process was used to meet another requirement only Function B had?"* Further discussion showed that Function B had another business requirement, which the current process partially addressed. At this point, there was only one question to address: *Could the current process also accommodate the requirement of Function B?*

As I read his message, funny thoughts occurred: *"If you (Function B) have stricter timelines than Function A, why don't you initiate the activities yourself?"* Little did I know that this simple thought would become a possibility and a reality a few months later.

You might remember the workflow process I described earlier: Function A initiates the process; the workflow continues to Function B and then goes back to Function A. That thought indicated the possibility of changing the accountabilities of specific activities from Function A to Function B.

Following the email exchange, I scheduled a meeting to follow up on the conversation. He freely expressed his views and concerns about the unacceptable timelines. I shared my thoughts on how this could be addressed and managed by transferring accountabilities from Function A to Function B. Unexpectedly, she (Function B) received the suggestion enthusiastically. She told me that Function B had wanted this for some time, although it was never raised or formally discussed within the process team. From our conversations, I could tell she had given much thought to this and had already pictured the updated process.

The implications of transferring accountability from Function A to Function B were phenomenal. When I first brought this up to Function A, he reacted with surprise and disbelief: *"Are you sure Function B will take these activities on? Of course, this would be great for us, but I don't think they will agree."* He didn't know what to believe. I responded, *"They have already agreed; in some ways, this was their idea."*

Discussions within the process team continued, and the benefits of this change for both functions became evident to all. I was convinced that transferring accountability would substantially simplify the process and address our challenges. I felt that the day-to-day activities of the end-users in Function B were closer to this process and that they would carry out these activities efficiently.

A transfer of accountability within a company often requires strong negotiation between the parties involved, as resources are a crucial aspect to consider. However, no negotiations took place; there was no need. This was a clear win-win situation where both parties enormously benefited.

What I like most about this story is how *"a concern"* expressed in an ordinary email went on an extraordinary journey to become a formal project with a fantastic outcome.

The bet

The idea grew within the process team, and its story evolved. The team contacted other stakeholders and informally discussed our intentions, emphasising the following statement: *"This change could lead to a considerable simplification of the current process."* One stakeholder was very excited and surprised by the news. *"Really?"* she said. *"I don't think Function B will accept accountability for this part of the process."*

At this point, I was confident that it was only a matter of time before the team implemented the change. To her statement, I added, *"I bet they will."* We agreed that a box of chocolates would be an adequate winning prize for the bet but did not associate any timelines with it; she probably thought she would win. The absence of timelines worked in my favour, as the project execution took slightly longer than I initially anticipated. As the project progressed, I returned to her several times with an offer to increase the bet-winning prize. However, she consistently rejected my proposal while facetiously accusing me of having privileged information. Oh well, I guess she was right!

A few weeks later, I received a lovely box of tasty chocolates shaped like a Christmas tree; it was December.

Starting from scratch

The two functions reached a formal agreement on the transfer of accountabilities with ease. This was not simply an exercise in updating the existing process but more like designing it from scratch.

I recall what a very experienced colleague once said: *"Every time there is an update to a process, we need to start from a clean sheet."* I couldn't agree more. Many process teams fail to grasp that a process update should not be an *"add-on"* exercise without further considerations; the process needs to be mapped out as if it were new.

This update required defining the main elements: the input that triggered the process, the output that signalled successful completion, and all the sub-activities. Clear roles and responsibilities were reassigned. The information we already had about the process was valuable; starting from a clean sheet does not imply ignoring what we already know.

Organisations must be vigilant to ensure that the process remains simple after implementation. However, this seems rather difficult for many, reminding me of the concept discussed earlier in the book: "the complexity bias" humans naturally exhibit. Because of complexity bias, many project participants want to make their mark with minor improvements or tweaks. These changes are typically minor, often unnecessary, and may initially appear benign. This accumulation happens slowly and usually goes unnoticed until it is too late. Suddenly, the process owners face an overly complicated process, asking how or when this happened. It is not that people intentionally want to make processes complex, but by introducing small, unnecessary changes and ignoring the bigger picture, they do!

Zooming in and out

In photographic terms, *"zoom in"* means making your subject more prominent in the frame without moving forward. On the other hand, to *"zoom out"* means making your subject smaller in the frame while viewing the surroundings. Zoom lenses allow you to do this and are incredibly convenient.

When working on business processes, I use the same terminology to explain where I am focusing. When I become interested in the details of a particular activity, I "zoom in." If I want to see how that activity fits into the overall process or, better yet, into the company's business objectives and goals (the bigger picture), I am "zooming out."

I have come across colleagues who were extremely talented and knowledgeable about a particular topic or activity; they loved the details. Many others could see the bigger picture, thinking about how specific actions can affect the overall success of a project or company; they found the details boring and distracting. Both types are crucial in-process work. Details are required for the end-users to perform a given task efficiently. However, a particular activity must make sense in the context of the process and, ultimately, the company's goals and objectives.

If you are one of those rare cases with the ability to "zoom in and out," you know this skill is handy in the corporate environment. You've probably noticed that this ability requires considerable mental energy, just like your camera would quickly run out of batteries if you keep zooming in and out on a specific subject or area of interest.

First things first

The new project began with the selection of team members, followed by the kick-off meeting. In this first meeting, the team agreed on project objectives, timelines, team expectations, and meeting frequency. The team decided to have biweekly meetings for the first two months. These meetings were beneficial as they facilitated collaboration, leadership, and sound decision-making among all team members.

Effective meetings

How the leader plans, prepares, executes, and follows up on each project meeting is critical to its success. Effective meetings generally have good energy, meaningful conversation, and constructive participant collaboration. They tend to be very interactive and valuable to all parties; they stick to the subject and use people's time and energy well.

Planning and Preparation: The first step is to formulate why we are meeting and what we are trying to accomplish. One might be tempted to draft an agenda right away, but defining the purpose of the meeting comes first. Then, drafting the agenda naturally follows. This phase requires being creative about the topics that need to be discussed and how to arrange the agenda in a logical order. Once the agenda is drafted, the identification of the participants comes next. It's puzzling why meeting organisers often include too many attendees. With a clear purpose and agenda, identifying who needs to be in the room to provide input, support, or expertise to reach the meeting goals should be straightforward.

You might think planning and preparation take time, and I couldn't agree more! However, does it pay off? It certainly does! Not investing time in this part of the process might lead to additional meetings to meet the same objectives, with no guarantee of success. Managing frustrated team members and possibly senior management is also an added challenge.

Execution: Effective meetings require strong leadership and facilitation skills. The organiser should set the tone, ensuring participants feel their time is well spent. The purpose and objectives of the meeting need to be established upfront. Another aspect is to stick to the points on the agenda. During discussions, unrelated but important topics may come up. In such cases, it's essential to acknowledge the relevance of those ideas and conversations but then set them aside in a *"meeting parking lot."* This is a way to document and keep track of essential items that may not be useful to discuss in the current meeting but may need to be addressed later. Effective meeting execution also requires managing participants' behaviours to avoid derailing the meeting; this is possibly the most challenging aspect of running meetings.

Summary and Follow-up

Accurate and timely meeting minutes are essential and often underestimated. They provide a clear record of what happened during the meeting, help hold people accountable, and facilitate the smooth implementation of decisions.

I remember a project team member once approached me after a meeting and said, *"The success of this project is due to how well-prepared the meetings are."* I added, *"I can't afford to end a meeting without achieving the goal or having participants confused or frustrated. I will do whatever I can to make it easy for the participants."*

The team discussed and made decisions on every aspect of the process design, with those documented on the slide deck at each meeting.

As mentioned, a strategy must be figured out well in advance for meetings to be effective. I recall many instances where I allocated hours to meeting planning and often reached out to participants in advance to get their thoughts and views on a particular aspect. By the time the meeting took place, most participants were fully aware of the subject under discussion and came to the meeting well-prepared. At each meeting, a simple and concise slide deck was presented. When a decision was required, the slide deck included the reason for the meeting goal first, background information, potential options with benefits and risks associated with each one, and a last empty slide with the heading *"Decision?"* This approach ensured that anyone new or external to the project could easily follow the sequence of events: what decisions were made, the rationale behind them, when, and by whom.

The team went through the mapping and design process as if it were new. As a result, the team identified further areas for enhancement that we would have otherwise missed. Surprisingly, those led to a significant process simplification of the current process. This is why a periodic end-to-end process review is considered a good practice, particularly if you hold *"keep it simple"* as the way to conduct your business.

The designing phase was completed, and an elegant and transparent process with well-defined shared accountabilities between two functions was created.

From decisions to instructions

The design of the future process resided on the meeting slides as diagrams and workflows, with footnote annotations and colourful boxes with text. There was only one thing left: transform the information on the slides into formal instructions for end-users to follow.

43

The team created procedural documents as a precise set of instructions that end-users could easily follow. This seemed like an effortless task, as the team made most decisions during previous phases of the project. However, as we were rewriting the procedural documents, we identified aspects that had not been addressed. Managing those situations during the write-up phase is as crucial as any other aspect of the process.

I remember when we missed addressing some minor but essential activities. This was identified during the writing phase, as the *"zoom-in"* lenses are on. I directed a question to the expert using the comment command within the document itself. She quickly responded with a simple statement, *"TBD"* (to be discussed). I smiled and nodded in agreement. She said, *"Let's meet to discuss this topic and get alignment."* A meeting was scheduled shortly after.

Why am I highlighting this aspect? Such questions often lead to lengthy discussions with many stakeholders within the document. Even though reaching a decision and getting alignment this way is possible, it is not a good practice. I have also seen emails written to get consensus or alignment among the recipients; these are ineffective, either. Regarding decision-making and ensuring alignment in a group, a formal team meeting, and post-meeting documentation are required.

Process vs. procedural documents

Process and procedural documents are not the same thing. A process describes a series of events leading to achieving a specific goal—a series of interconnected steps that lead to a particular outcome. On the other hand, a procedural document provides systematic, detailed instructions for end-to-end users to follow. A process focuses on a high-level overview, the bigger picture, whereas a procedure is a low-level description with specific instructions and expected actions.

In my opinion, a procedural document is simply the documentation of a procedure and the final output end-users use to perform their activities. I often find processes that are straightforward in principle but described in such a confusing manner that end-users cannot follow them. Many wrongly say this process is complex, whereas the only complexity is how the process is written and documented.

A short detour

I remember discussing the need to create a business process in a company. After some debating, senior management decided, and a project team was assembled with participants from different functions. During the kick-off meeting, one of the project participants immediately remarked: *"Let's write a standard operating procedure (SOP); we need the template."*

Unfortunately, this is a common practice followed by many companies. How a decision to create a business process could immediately follow a procedural document write-up without discussions or decisions on the workflow and description of roles and responsibilities still puzzles me. This is a clear case of a procedural document used as the vehicle to manage the decision-making process. These ineffective shortcuts result in confusion and frustration among the team members due to inefficient decision-making and a lack of proper documentation.

<u>Back to the story</u>

The team produced clear instructions in procedural documents with the information collected on the slide decks. The written style was appropriate, using imperative mood, short sentences, specific statements, and placing the most critical aspect at the beginning of a sentence. With this simple format, I was sure end-users would consult the procedural documents instead of implementing their best practices or shortcuts.

Summary and Lessons

See the sequence of events in the story below:

1. Errors are identified, and deviations are reported.

2. Corrective and preventive measures are in place.

3. The effectiveness of the measures implemented was partially passed.

4. The team identifies areas for enhancement.

5. A process internal audit takes place.

6. Discussions pushed the team back to the start.

7. Function B expresses a concern to the team by email.

8. Function B formulates a second business requirement.

9. Functions A and B meet to discuss.

10. The team agrees that the current process absorbs the new business requirement from B.

11. The process is redesigned.

12. Senior management endorses the new process.

13. Procedural documents are rewritten.

This was another of those incredible journeys with one pivotal moment—just an ordinary email that fundamentally changed the way this process would be managed in the future.

Lessons Learned

- Remain Flexible: Flexibility allows you to respond quickly to changing circumstances. If the wheel already exists, don't reinvent it!

- Don't forget your end-users: Anticipate the challenges for end-users; if the process doesn't make achieving the end goals easy, it's not fit for purpose.

- Be vigilant and open: Many ways exist to simplify processes and change to efficient working methods. Be watchful when everyone is sleeping!

- Question your own beliefs and assumptions: The impossible only exists in the minds of those who see the future as an extrapolation of the past.

- Be pragmatic in your problem-solving approach: Dig at the roots instead of just hacking at the leaves!

- Speak your mind: *Your opinion matters*!

- Meet, discuss, decide, document, and formalise.

In our story, the team created the procedural documents after the process workflow with defined roles and responsibilities agreed upon and endorsed by senior management.

No shortcuts allowed; follow the process!

CHAPTER 4

ARE YOU TALKING TO ME?

Communication has always been one of my favourite subjects. Even in my childhood, I found that the ability to anticipate outcomes gave me plenty of time to prepare my arguments for or against whatever topic was up for discussion. I used those skills when communicating or negotiating with my parents, siblings, and friends. They often found me obnoxious, as they were usually caught off guard and without words. My arguments brought me success, and I frequently felt I won the debate.

Effective communication is one of the most valuable skills when navigating the complexities of a multi-layered corporate structure. It becomes essential when leading multidisciplinary projects or representing functions or disciplines in a project team.

As previously discussed, preparation is critical for an effective meeting, yet it is often neglected. I frequently observe leaders rushing into meetings unprepared, starting with the statement, "I apologise; I did not have much time to prepare for this meeting." This can occasionally happen for many reasons, but the problem is when it becomes the norm in day-to-day operations. Every time this occurs, the same thing comes to mind: "If you do not have time to prepare for the meeting now, you might have to make time to fix the misunderstandings and disagreements that may arise later on!"

In this section, I will share my thoughts and views on effective communication, what it means, and how poor communication can create a tense environment where people are not motivated to be productive and are not inspired to collaborate.

The way words travel

The belief that we communicate well is a widespread assumption. Even when we suspect someone might not grasp what we are saying, we might fall into the trap of thinking this has to do with them rather than with us. If an individual (A) explains something to an individual (B) and individual (B) does not understand it, who is accountable? Let's dive into the sequence of events from the moment we think we want to communicate to what others understand: Individual A (speaker) talks to individual B (listener).

A thinks…

A says...

B hears...

B understands...

<u>What individual A thinks and says:</u>

Thinking is an essential mental process. It helps us define and organize experiences, plan, learn, reflect, and create. It is simply a product of the mind and a repository of thoughts and ideas accumulated over a lifetime. However, thoughts and ideas only get into a linear format when we speak aloud or write. The conversion of thoughts into words and sentences happens automatically, almost unconsciously. The words we select to convey the message are essential; they must be precise and accurately represent what we think we want to say. It is often the case that what we think we want to say and what we say are not 100% aligned. "Apologies, this is not what I meant to say. Let me rephrase!" you might have heard on occasion. This level of self-awareness is rare, but it can happen.

Another interesting scenario occurs when the listener does not speak a language fluently but may have some basic knowledge of grammar and understanding. This reminds me of my early days in the UK. I often reached out to the most-used sentence when interacting with the locals: "*I do not understand.*" In such situations, the speaker took different approaches to help me understand what they were trying to say (or they thought they were helping):

- Repetition of the same sentence with no variation.

- Repetition of the same sentence but louder. "There must be confusion between not understanding something and being deaf," I thought.

- Repetition of the same sentence but, this time, exceptionally slowly. This approach rarely helped, not to mention how awkward the slow speech sounded.

Once I became fluent in English, I observed other foreigners facing identical situations; it was amusing. What puzzled me was that the speaker used the *exact* words, repeatedly expecting a different outcome. By using synonymous words or breaking the sentence into smaller parts and checking with the listener, you would think the chances of getting the message across would be higher, right? It seems that was not obvious.

Returning to the main topic, we can agree that subtleties exist between thought and speech and that assuming they are the same is wrong.

<u>What individual B hears and understands:</u>

When the speaker communicates, they assume that the listener is paying full attention, the speech is clear, the grammar is perfect, and there are no distractions or cultural differences between the two parties involved. However, the reality may be somewhat different. The listener may only capture some incoming sound vibrations, whereas other parts are missed. Therefore, information entering the listener's hearing system could be slightly distorted and present gaps compared to what the speaker's phonatory system emits.

As sounds enter the hearing system, the listener processes the sound vibrations through historical filters of mental models or personal beliefs, converting them into signals that match existing circuits. The brain skilfully discards those that do not fit the model and makes a subjective interpretation of the original message. We could agree that because of how information enters the hearing system and is processed by the listener, the message may differ slightly from what the speaker initially intended.

Based on this model, there are ways in which project leaders or managers could minimize the risk of misalignment and potential confusion. One of them is presenting the message to the audience in a concise and straightforward style. By doing so, the speaker ensures that what they say (a written message) reflects what they want to say, provided enough time is allowed to formulate the message.

What the listener receives (this time visually) also matches the information transmitted by the speaker. Therefore, this approach effectively avoids potential misunderstandings arising from steps 1, 2, and 3, whereas step 4 can be handled by requesting feedback or confirmation from the audience.

In summary, I would like to emphasize a quote that some of you might have heard before: "Effective communication is not what you say; it is what the other person hears." However, based on what I have discussed, we could go one step further: "Effective communication is not what you think you want to say; it is what the other person understands."

The other side of the river

There is another famous quote that I wanted to bring: "I am responsible only for what I say, not for what you understand." We are responsible for our actions, words, feelings, and emotions; no one else is. However, the accountability of leaders should go beyond this if you are committed to achieving your project goals and objectives. As a project leader, the assumption that all team members fully understand what you communicate at meetings, for example, is risky. A better strategy may be the opposite: assume there will always be at least one participant who does not fully understand.

For this reason, leaders need to plan their meeting strategy carefully to maximize the chances of meeting success and avoid confusion or misunderstandings. As already mentioned, one possibility is to present a message to the audience in a concise writing style. Use slides; do not just talk. I follow this approach in any meeting I chair, regardless of the objectives or goals, and it seems to work. When the message is available in writing to the audience (i.e., on a single slide), one ensures alignment between what you want to say, what you say, and what the audience receives (reads, in this case). Remember to allocate enough time to formulate the message so the audience understands it.

Based on these observations, here are some recommendations and other considerations that I feel can lead to meeting success when using presentation slides:

- Formulate the message concisely. A few bullet points are enough. Choose your words carefully and use short sentences, as if you were writing a telegram (imagine a cost associated with each word). Avoid filler and buzz words and phrases. Take your time to think and ensure that what you want to say aligns with what you say or write.

- Use animations. Consider bringing up one sentence or section on the screen at a time. This is an effective way to keep readers focused and engaged, as anticipation keeps readers reading. As those text boxes appear on the screen sequentially, you might want to read them aloud one by one once the reader has time to do so. Alternatively, you could paraphrase or complement the written text with additional thoughts, ideas, or background, but only after the audience has finished reading.

- Use silence as a call for attention and focus; over speaking is unnecessary.

- Check with the audience. Invite questions, request feedback, and ask for opinions. Occasionally, I follow up with some attendees after the meeting to ensure that nothing is missed and there is alignment.

- Structure your presentation logically. For example, if you are seeking alignment on a particular subject or course of action, a few slides are enough: 1-question, 2-background, 3-4 options and points to consider for each, and 5-decision.

Other aspects of slide presentations can influence the audience's ability to follow and understand a message: font type and style, location of text boxes, diagrams, or tables on the slide, colours to use, and when. In addition, who the participants are and to what function or group they belong are also important. If you are familiar with the attendees' ways of thinking and working, why not facilitate their understanding process and adapt the presentation accordingly?

All this may seem obvious; however, I have attended many presentations where the speaker used crammed slides. It seemed there was no time to prepare, and the leader wrote the first thing that came to mind. How can the audience be ignored in this way?

However, this still occurs even when the time to prepare is available. I struggle to identify a single benefit of having busy slides; still, most presentations are full of them. What is even more interesting to watch is how those creating such presentations genuinely enjoy a more straightforward style and see the benefits when those are presented. However, many seem to struggle when creating them themselves.

Presenting busy slides has no benefits; to the contrary, the audience might not be able to read them or spend a long time doing so. While the audience reads them, they are not listening to the speaker; our conscious attention can only focus on one or the other (although it can absorb certain information). How often have you felt your heart sink as soon as the first slide appeared on the screen? You probably switched your focus from the presentation to your mobile screen or something else in anticipation of a long and painful presentation. In addition, the text often sounds lacking in conviction, and the presenter gets an initial negative feeling from the audience, which might put them off attending future presentations.

As discussed before, proper preparation requires significant energy and time. You probably think you do not have time to invest in this level of preparation due to other conflicting priorities. If so, you might consider revisiting your priority list and reshuffling it. No one likes to feel they are wasting time, and often, participants leave the room confused and frustrated, thinking that nothing was achieved. Worse, the team makes a wrong decision due to a lack of clarity or misunderstanding.

This is hugely costly for companies, as you could find yourself back in the room with the same colleagues discussing the same topics a few months later and with everyone wondering why or how this happened.

Many years ago, I got my first job at a big company. A project was set up to address some regulatory requirements and managed by a team and a senior leader. This project had been ongoing for years without achieving any of its objectives. One day, I was invited to attend an important meeting where the project leader and team presented to senior management. I do not remember why I got this invitation, but I happily accepted it. I was eager to learn more about this project's progress and why it had been stagnant for a long time.

Everything made sense right from the start of the meeting when I noticed the presentation was 35 slides long. My heart stopped when the first slide appeared on the screen, and I bet others felt the same way. The slide was crammed with content, and the font size was too small to read. *"It is not going to work,"* I thought. I do not recall all the meeting specifics, but I remember that the presenter did not make it past the first few slides after the one-hour presentation. Senior management constantly interrupted her, with most discussions stuck around wordsmithing; the point of the meeting was lost from the start. Once the meeting ended, the team left the room frustrated and disappointed and blamed everybody else for their failure. I am not sure they understood what the problem was. *How can someone of that level of seniority get it so wrong?* I asked myself. I was still young and naïve, with an idyllic view of the corporate environment.

This may seem incredible to you, but it can get worse. I remember many occasions when the speaker said, "Apologies for this busy slide. What this slide means to show is..." This remark always strikes me, and the same thoughts come to mind: "Knowing that the slide is busy and that the audience will struggle to understand it, do you still show it? Why would you want to do this?" The answer to these questions remains unknown. At this point, you may think, "People have different styles when presenting." To me, there is only one acceptable style when presenting: the style that works.

Soon after this experience, the company appointed me as the project leader for a different initiative. Some months into the project, the team reached the first milestone and prepared a presentation to senior management. The project sponsor (who happened to be the same one as in the project mentioned above) approached me with a request: *"I would like you to present to me before the meeting with the senior team. And please, ensure you make the presentation simple with no more than 15 slides."* I understood he was trying to minimise the risk of the same situation happening again. I responded with surprise and disbelief: "*I have prepared six slides, but if you would like, I can add more information.*" The rest is history, perhaps for another time.

My approach to presentations and communication, in general, has evolved over the years. However, already in my childhood, I had some understanding of what "this business" of communication was about: "The more words you say or write, the more chances you might get something wrong, and people will pick on you."

Communication is now all and only about the audience. It is not what I want to say that is important, but instead, what I want listeners to understand; it is not the same. When there is a focus change from oneself to others, when you change perspective, everything changes, including your entire life. You might remember earlier in the book when I shared my response to a colleague's remark: "*I cannot afford to end a meeting without having the goal achieved or having participants confused or frustrated. I will do whatever I can to make it easy for the participants.*"

Nice to have

In a business setting, "nice-to-have" items are non-essential aspects that could make a business or working environment more attractive but will not prevent the business from functioning normally. Conversely, a "must" in business refers to elements essential for providing products or services or meeting regulatory requirements. This concept extends beyond business to other areas of life. For example, when a team writes a procedural document or prepares a presentation, some team members often suggest adding text or steps because they are "nice to have."

At the heart of effective communication lies a simple question: does the information benefit the audience? Including non-essential text in technical documents and presentations can introduce unnecessary complexity, undermining the intended goals and objectives. This is a stark reminder of prioritizing the audience's needs over personal preferences or 'nice-to-have' elements.

I want to highlight a topic: *the process of writing*. As already described, thinking is a product of the mind, a repository of thoughts, ideas, and experiences in a multidimensional space in our brains. Once the intention to communicate appears, these thoughts unconsciously shape into a linear structure. When the message is in writing, it gives us time to reflect and adjust it to become effective.

Once the draft message is on paper, the focus should shift from oneself to the audience. This phase involves discarding non-essentials, rephrasing and tweaking, choosing concise words, and other considerations described earlier. This activity is like spring cleaning: redecorating, reshuffling, and throwing away junk. In both situations, discarding the "non-essentials" seems challenging.

For many years, as part of my job, I have reviewed documents requiring lists of steps and concise instructions, including scientific papers and regulatory, procedural, and strategic documents. I often find these poorly written, which explains why many end-users might not follow them.

I have put a set of instructions together to illustrate what I commonly find when I review such documents. (A) represents the original text, and (B) provides suggestions for alternative text.

Role	A- Activities	B- Alternative
A	Acquire the report template ~~to write the report~~	Write the report using the template
A	Write the report ~~with all information available.~~	
A	~~Review the report to ensure all the information has been incorporated.~~	
A	Send ~~the completed~~ report to B	Send the report to B by email
B	~~When the report is received from A,~~ file it in ~~the appropriate project folder.~~	Receive the document and file it in Y.
B	~~After filling out the document,~~ notify C that the document is ready for review and provide ~~instructions on where the report is~~	Notify C that the document is ready for review by email. Provide link
C	Review the report ~~after receiving a notification that it is ready for review.~~	Review the report
C	~~Immediately after reviewing the report,~~ email it back to A ~~for finalization.~~	Send the document to A by email.
A	Address comments ~~received in the report~~	Address comments and finalize
A	~~After addressing comments,~~ finalize the report.	
A	Distribute it to all relevant stakeholders by email	Distribute it to the stakeholders by email

I have grouped the errors above into six categories depending on their nature:

1. Stating the Obvious:

Write the report with all the information available.

Address comments received in the report.

After addressing comments, finalize the report.

2.Stating the Reason for Activities:

Review the report to ensure all the information has been incorporated.

3.Instructions are not Specific Enough:

File it in the appropriate project folder. (Which one?) Send the report to B. (How?)

4.Long and Wordy Sentences:

Provide instructions on where the report is.

5.Unnecessary Split of Activities:

Address comments received in the report. After addressing comments, finalize the report.

The two activities described as independent tasks can be combined into one short sentence.

6.Unnecessary Use of Words::

Distribute it to all relevant stakeholders by email.

The word "relevant" is inappropriate in this context. "Do you know of any non-relevant stakeholders?". How about the word "all"?

The suggestions represent a simplification of the instructions in the above table. The process itself has not changed. However, the description is simple, easy to follow, and facilitates end-user execution. A well-written technical document reminds me of a "cooking recipe," but the cook performs all of them without any roles assigned to the activities. See below a recipe taken from a cookbook:

- Cook the rice in a large saucepan of boiling water for 12 minutes or until tender.

- Drain and leave to cool.

- Heat oil in a non-stick wok or large frying pan over medium heat.

- Add eggs and swirl over the base to form an omelette. Cook for 2 minutes or until set.

- Transfer to a chopping board. Set aside to cool slightly. Roll up and thickly slice.

- Add bacon to the wok. Cook for 4 minutes until lightly golden.

- Add carrots. Stir-fry for 1 minute.

- Add shallots, peas, and rice. Cook, stirring for 3-4 minutes.

- Add egg and soy sauce. Stir until heated through.

- Sprinkle with sesame seeds and top with extra shallots. Serve immediately.

Shall we have a little fun by making the first activity in the recipe unnecessarily complex?

- ✓ Take a saucepan, add water, put it on the stove (high heat), and wait until the water is boiling. Only then (and not before) add the rice to the saucepan and wait 12 minutes. You might also test the rice and stop cooking it when you realize it is tender.

What people need to know

In previous sections, I have discussed the importance of effective communication and provided tips and techniques for mastering one of the most sought-after workplace skills. In principle, effective communication should be automatic. However, when we communicate with others, something can go astray; we might say one thing, the other person hears something else, and misunderstandings, frustration, and conflicts arise. This is well understood in business, which is why strategic communication plans began.

Communication plans are strategic documents that outline objectives, key messages, channels, and communication activities, including timelines. The most important aspect is setting clear goals and objectives. Does the message intend to inform or persuade? Does it require collaboration from others? Developing an effective plan is impossible if what we try to achieve is not defined. Yet, this happens often, and it is here where things can go wrong.

See below the most common objectives of communication plans, together with suggestions on how to make them effective.

- Inform: Informative plans provide an audience with information and resources, often used to raise awareness or educate others about a topic. The message and key components must encompass simple facts and words, be easy to understand, and not be excessively long. Would you read a long email on a topic intended only for your awareness? I should probably read them!

- Persuade: Persuasive plans require messages to encourage an audience to take action. For example, advising employees to complete compulsory training or to follow a procedural document are examples of persuasive messages. They include arguments and stories to convince people. Indeed, the audience might not always receive these messages positively, and feelings get hurt along the way. Still, the tone may be adapted so the message does not sound harsh or demotivating.

- Collaborate: Collaborative plans are required when planning and executing projects alongside each other are necessary. This particular plan type requires clear goals and objectives and getting everyone engaged and on board. An example is communicating a regulatory inspection outcome when there are critical or significant findings. In such a situation, a project team forms, and its members are held accountable for all communication activities.

Effective communication should be spontaneous, with common sense as the main working principle. However, after working in different companies, I can only wonder. See below some of the most common errors or oversights I have observed over the years.

- Lack of clear and well-defined objectives: We will lack direction and focus on the message if we do not know what or why we communicate. The one-size-fits-all approach does not work.

- Lack of a clear message: Companies often communicate with mixed messages or overly complex corporate jargon, leading to confusion among the target audience. It is true that "less is always more," but not providing enough information can result in a failure to achieve the intended goal. Provide the correct amount of information. Concise and thoughtful communications resonate with readers and are the best way to engage your audience. Start with the main point, as this may be the audience's only reading. The background can follow in subsequent bullet points. Keep it short.

- Poorly designed or unattractive content: You may have well-written and concise text, but it will lose effectiveness if presented with a lousy design or layout. Visual content is essential, as people are likelier to remember information presented in a visual format than text alone. Using infographics, engaging images, attractive font styles, and exciting colours helps.

- Limited communication channels: Some years ago, I suggested the project team schedule a Q&A session with process end-users to address their thoughts and concerns about the process. I recall that a team member was surprised, and by her reaction, I concluded that this was an unusual thing to do.

- Wrong communication timing, with information shared too late or too early: I have seen projects up and running without an adequate communication plan. Then, as the team starts discussing end-user learning and training, they realize that the project needs visibility. Conversely, some may want to communicate before anything is done on the project. Getting the communication timing right is challenging but not impossible. It makes sense to start low-key, introducing the project to the intended audience and communicating the goals and objectives. Then, communicate any milestones achieved as they happen, explaining their importance and the next steps. You might notice that your intended audience receives your messages with interest and credibility, and trust is built over time. Also, adjust the communication plan in real time, as unforeseen events can occur.

- Failing to tailor communication: The message needs to consider differences within the intended audience, such as roles, responsibilities, and levels of expertise.

- Setting wrong expectations: assuming that changes or stories excite everyone. We must consider that even positive news (such as process simplification) can initially be stressful.

Another aspect I would like to highlight is the lack of realization that leaders should model good communication practices. I have encountered many with poor verbal and writing skills and lacking creativity or intuition in their presentation abilities. Junior employees might adopt these habits and accept them as the norm.

In summary, communicating and speaking are not the same thing. Communicating refers to successfully transmitting a message, whereas speaking is uttering words to get it across; sometimes, it works, and sometimes, it does not. The question is simple: Are you talking, or are you communicating?

Summary and Lessons

- Invest time in preparation.

  Allocate enough time to think and adequately articulate the intended message. If you do not invest the energy and time now, you might have to allocate it later.

  Prepare, prepare, and prepare!

- Know the audience.

  Find out who your audience is—their background, function, or groups they belong to. This will help you better plan and allow you to speak their language, highlighting what matters to them.

  Wear other shoes!

- Keep your goals and objectives present.

  If your objective is to ensure the audience understands a specific topic or message, then your communication strategy should reflect that. Remember, it is not about you; it is about the audience.

  Your goals are about you; the rest is not!

- Use clear and concise language.

  Make your point with the fewest words possible. Proofread over what you have written and look for places to cut down words and sentences. Avoid the use of corporate jargon.

  Simple is good!

- Exercise creativity and intuition.

Start your presentation with a story that resonates with the audience; the audience will be engaged and want to know more. Use impactful pictures, as they arouse emotions and provoke thought.

Storytelling is the heartbeat of any presentation!

- Self-reflection.

  After the meeting, reflect on your communication or presentation skills. You could have done better if the audience did not understand your message.

  Learn now and apply next time around!

- Request feedback.

  Ask for honest feedback on your communication skills with relevant and objective perspectives from people you trust.

  Look for your blind spots!

CHAPTER 5

OF PROJECT TEAMS AND OTHER THINGS

I am sure you're familiar with the concept of project teams. A project team typically consists of a project manager or leader and a group of individual team members, including yourself, who work together to achieve a project's goals. Your responsibilities are crucial, including collaborating with the project lead or manager throughout the project life cycle, completing assigned deliverables, and meeting all requirements. You also contribute significantly to the team's overall performance and keep the project leader or manager informed of the project's progress. Your potential solutions are vital to the group's consideration when facing challenges.

Throughout my years of attending project team meetings in various roles, such as project manager, subject matter expert, business process owner, and project leader, I have witnessed and experienced multiple team dynamics and situations involving leaders and managers. While team behaviour is often discussed in books and scientific papers, it's surprising that little information is available on dysfunctional leaders or managers. The focus is usually on dysfunctional teams. I find this discrepancy intriguing and wonder why it is the case.

In theory, we could spend hours discussing why some teams fail to function as expected and how to improve their performance through effective management. However, based on my experience, I believe that the root cause of erratic team behaviour often boils down to one simple fact: the team is led by a dysfunctional leader.

In this chapter, I aim to delve into the various aspects of project teams, including their leaders or managers and their behaviours. Drawing from my first-hand experience and practical observations, I will share my thoughts and views on this subject. By exploring the role of leaders and managers within project teams, we can gain valuable insights into how their behaviour influences team dynamics and overall project success. This knowledge can inspire and motivate us, including you, to grow and improve in our leadership roles, fostering personal and professional development.

It is about you

Years ago, I found myself in a unique situation. Despite my role at the time not requiring any formal leadership or managerial skills, I had the opportunity to attend a one-day internal leadership skills course organized by the corporation I worked for. I was curious and decided to participate. The course began with the consultant introducing himself to the group, followed by individual introductions from all attendees. We were asked to share details about our professional backgrounds and explain why we had chosen to attend the course.

Out of all the participants, there was one individual whose reason for being there stood out to me. She expressed that working with her team had become challenging. She felt alienated by her team and shared how this manifested in their day-to-day activities. She hoped that this course would equip her with the necessary tools and insights to perform her job effectively and meet the expectations of others.

As she shared her experiences with the group, I immediately understood why she had enrolled in the course. Her words were thought-provoking, and her tone and body language conveyed a sense of provocation. "I hope she learns a few things here," I thought.

As the workshop progressed, the consultant presented various aspects of the managerial role (though the exact details escape my memory). There was a lively and friendly exchange of ideas among the attendees until she boldly challenged the consultant, declaring, "I do not agree with you; I do not think it works this way." The room fell into an awkward silence. This situation remains so vivid in my memory because her remarks and assertiveness took me aback. I couldn't fathom how someone could challenge an expert with years of experience in such a manner. Her comments caught the consultant off guard, yet he managed to navigate the uncomfortable situation without exposing anyone. At that moment, the consultant began to understand why she had chosen to attend the course and the challenges her team faced. It's akin to attending a cooking course and having one of the students confidently tell the teacher they are incorrect in a cooking technique or approach. It's shocking!

In such circumstances, many individuals, particularly those who do not grasp the concept of leadership or management, may label her team as dysfunctional. However, in my opinion, this is rarely the case. When a team fails to perform effectively, it is often a sign of poor leadership. Her lack of empathy and self-awareness made the obvious apparent.

Self-awareness

Awareness is knowing that something exists and having a conscious understanding of what is happening in our surroundings in the present moment. Oxford English defines self-awareness as the conscious knowledge of one's character, feelings, motives, and desires. It involves understanding oneself and identifying weaknesses, strengths, triggers, and motivators. Self-awareness allows individuals to monitor, focus, and control their emotions and reactions, making it a valuable skill in various aspects of life, including business.

Tasha Eurich and her research team conducted a large-scale scientific study on self-awareness. The study involved ten independent investigations with approximately 5,000 participants. The results were intriguing, revealing that only 10% to 15% of the participants met the criteria for "self-awareness." This finding challenges the common belief that most people are self-aware. It suggests that true self-awareness is a rare quality.

Though most people believe they are self-aware, you may be surprised that only 10%—15% of the people under study fit the "self-awareness" criteria. If we go back to the story, you would agree that the course participant in question had low levels of self-awareness. She probably had some understanding of it as she agreed with her management to attend this course (although Human Resources (HR) could have made it mandatory for continuation in that role; I do not know). That is as far as I would go. I think she knew little about how *others perceived and received her*. When egos get in the way, self-awareness is hindered.

It is important to note that self-awareness is not just about introspection. It involves being present in the moment, observing one's thoughts, feelings, and actions, and understanding how they align with internal standards. By developing self-awareness, individuals can make more informed decisions and navigate the complex and ever-changing business environment more effectively.

Self-awareness is crucial for understanding oneself, relating to others, and making sound decisions. While it may be a rare quality, it is a skill that can be cultivated and developed over time.

It is not about you

Many years ago, I was assigned the project lead/manager role in a program running for a few months. The previous manager had left the company, but not before handing over a colossal amount of information with all sorts of details. I was overwhelmed but decided to go with the flow, at least initially. I scheduled the first meeting to introduce myself and review the goals and objectives with the team. However, soon after the meeting started, I sensed something was not quite right.

You must have heard the expression - the elephant in the room! I can assure you that it felt like a herd of elephants then! Discussions began, and I felt the intense frustration of some participants, whereas others seemed to have come to terms with 'whatever it was' not resonating with them. I found the situation unusual and was curious to know why or what the issues with this project and team were. I understand that disagreements and conflicts often occur between people with different perspectives, personalities, and experiences, but I felt this was something else.

By the end of the meeting, I had a plan: I scheduled meetings with every team member and encouraged them to speak honestly. The following week was busy with daily meetings; "*what we say here, it stays here*" was the starting line. As their personalities were different, so were their attitudes. Some were polite, emotions drove others, and some very assertively expressed their frustrations. As discussions progressed, I noticed a common theme appearing in all the discussions: it all came down to one simple fact. At that moment, the reasons for the team's frustrations became clear to me, and not only that, but I also felt their feelings were justified. As it turned out, this was a case of two overlapping projects ongoing simultaneously, without cross-communication — not unusual in big companies built on silos. I will not describe what happened next, but I can tell you that

I scheduled a second and final team meeting a few weeks later to close out the project and say goodbye. Participants were delighted because they were heard and did not have to waste time and energy on something they found unnecessary. I remember referring to "no one likes feeling they are wasting time" earlier in the book, right?

Team trust

Trust is at the core of high-performing teams and often focuses on the relationship between managers and employees. A lack of confidence can result in fear of conflict, the creation of silos, a lack of effective communication, or the micromanagement of the team. When trust exists between peers and the leader, there is less friction and more collaboration. In the story I described, I truly appreciated the members' honesty at our meetings. With their honest feedback, I identified the root cause of their frustration and acted promptly while deciding on the next steps.

Alternatively, the project could have continued to be active for months while managed by an unfriendly and frustrated team. I am not sure I would have survived this setting for long! The outcome of the investigation was to the benefit of everyone and the company, too.

Do you need to be there?

Selecting meeting attendees is vital to leading productive meetings, but its importance is still significantly undermined. Meeting attendees should be those who can add value to a meeting or a specific item on the agenda. However, many project leaders do not apply this principle when scheduling meetings. Generally, there is the illusion that the more people attend a meeting, the greater the collaboration will be when this could not be further from the truth. In addition, there is the concept of "complexity bias," which we discussed earlier in the book. There is the wrong perception that significant projects require many participants and that they all must simultaneously be involved in the same way. Also, there is the perception that the more colleagues participate in a project or a meeting, the more prominent or relevant they are.

Selecting meeting attendees is like choosing teammates for a football match. Would you select five defenders when three may be enough? Would you choose a player only because he wants to play, even though he has not demonstrated the highest ability or commitment to the team?

If you ask a football coach why a player is not in the starting line-up of a match, he probably provides you with a well-thought-out reason why this is the case. However, this is often not the case when discussing meeting participation (who should attend). Some of the rationales for inviting a colleague are as unhelpful as "just in case," "because he needs to know certain aspects," or "because I was not sure, then I decided to include him." When someone says, "*I have invited them just in case,*" I always hope they finish the sentence in a way that would clarify further. However, they never do; that is the end. Those who invite someone to a meeting because they need to know may be correct if the conference's objective is to inform. The problem comes when the objective is different, for example, when addressing an issue and making decisions. There are many ways to inform and update stakeholders on project progress or challenges; they do not have to attend meetings with different objectives.

Many leaders would instead invite someone than take the risk of potentially missing something important, even if the presence of others minimizes the risk. In addition, others may make strategic decisions by playing the political game. I am sure you know what I am referring to. Either way, inviting more people than required to a meeting seems the safest bet for many, like adding unnecessary words to a procedural document or slides. I consider both the unnecessary words and unnecessary participants in a meeting as "non-essentials." We make our lives unnecessarily complicated whenever we reach out to "non-essentials" and "nice to haves." I felt this way when I carried a 15-kg backpack on my last trip to South America when 8 kg would have done the job nicely!

Many years ago, I led a multidisciplinary project team assembled to address a new business requirement. The project had been ongoing for some time, and we had reached a critical milestone where endorsement by senior management was required. The team prepared a very focused but high-level presentation tailored to the needs of senior management (as you know, they generally have little time and no interest in specific details). One team member was transitioning to another project, and I knew who his replacement was. However, this was not yet official. A few days before the presentation, a future team member reached out to me to chat, and she had a request: "*It would be nice if I could attend the meeting to find out what is going on in the project.*" I am sure many of you would have welcomed her to the meeting without hesitation; after all, she just wanted to sit and listen, right?

However, I did hesitate. I felt that it would have been the wrong thing to do and for several good reasons. Inviting her to the meeting would have confused the team, as the new assignment and starting date were unknown. In addition, it would have sent the wrong message as not all team members participated; only those directly involved in the topic attended. Also, I doubted she would have understood much of the topic and the discussions during the meeting. She would have concluded that the project was complex and convoluted when, in reality, it was not.

Her immense enthusiasm and proactivity were commendable, and I was sorry to hear about her disappointment when I shared my position and arguments with her. She was probably caught off guard because the company culture was "inclusion-regardless" rather than "inclusion-if-all benefits." As a project leader, my loyalty is always with the team, making the best decisions for their benefit and avoiding any situation that can generate confusion. This was simply a case of who needed to attend a meeting and why. In addition, I feel that leaving someone out of a meeting shows consideration for another person's time and should not be regarded as disrespectful.

Instead, I offered her an introductory, focused session with me so I could share all the information I thought she needed. We met later that same week, and she said that, on reflection, she understood the rationale behind the decision and was looking forward to working on this project. I was delighted! On a different note, the meeting went well; it was very efficient, and we achieved a positive outcome. I communicated to all project team members straight after the meeting with information on how the meeting went, topics discussed, and feedback from senior management.

I have just addressed the participation of people in project meetings. However, what about the number of participants in a project? This may seem like a different story, but the same principles apply. In big companies, it is typical for a project team to be cross-functional or to include people from other teams. Depending on the project type, the number of experts required to participate may be overwhelmingly high, but this does not mean all of them must be in the room simultaneously.

I remember once being assigned another of those projects that had been running for years without getting closer to achieving any goals and objectives. A first meeting occurred, and I introduced myself as the new project lead. I do not recall precisely how many participants were on the call, but more than 15. Why so many? *"Having this number of participants in every meeting will not work!"* I remember thinking to myself. The team consisted of experts with varying skills, abilities, and experience; they all needed to be involved. I also recognized some names from prior interactions with other projects or initiatives.

During the first meeting, I took on more of an observer role, paying attention to the team dynamics and personalities of the team members. It did not take long before my sneaking suspicions were confirmed: the setup of this project is neither practical nor efficient. In the next few days, I scheduled several meetings with familiar participants to discover why the project was stuck and the challenges and obstacles.

The feedback from these discussions echoed a common challenge: the previous project leader. I won't delve into the specifics of his departure here. My first step was to reorganize the participants into two groups: the designers, the content experts, and the execution team, the implementation experts. The designers included all functional subject matter experts, with the sponsor and other external advisors joining as ad-hoc members. The execution team comprised change managers, training experts, and procedural document writers.

During the second meeting, I shared the new project setup with the team, and they all welcomed the change. That was the last time all 15+ participants were in the room together until the closeout meeting a few months later. We agreed on timelines and deliverables for each group and that the second team would get involved only after the first group had met the objectives.

It's important to note that the new project setup didn't mean the execution team was left in the dark during the initial phase or that the designers were unaware of the progress once they had completed their part, which was far from it. We maintained regular email communications with all project members, providing updates on the progress, challenges, potential delays, and their reasons.

The designer's team immediately delved into discussions, demonstrating their readiness and enthusiasm. Managing a team meeting of 6 to 8 participants was a breeze, fostering focused and productive conversations. The team's diligence paid off as they swiftly achieved the first milestone: a meticulously designed process poised for the sponsor and senior management's endorsement. Despite some controversial discussions, the execution team was primed to take over the project, marking the beginning of the second phase. A mere ten months after my initial meeting with the team, the new process was successfully implemented in the organisation, a testament to the team's efficiency and effectiveness.

Effectiveness and efficiency

These two words are used interchangeably without fully appreciating what they truly mean. Focusing too much on one and not the other could be problematic. In simple terms, effectiveness refers to what you do—accomplishing the right thing—whereas efficiency refers to how you do it—time and effort allocated. In the business process environment, equality is important. Generally, a project may fail due to two underlying issues: the goals and objectives are not clearly defined (what to do) and not delivered on time or with the quality required (how you do it).

For example, when the authorities release a new regulatory requirement, most, if not all, companies implement it by the required deadline. However, how this is achieved may result in a significant drain on resources or gaps in quality. In this case, one could say that the business process is adequate but not efficient.

For projects to succeed, the teams need to be practical and efficient, with effectiveness coming first. What is the point of using limited resources to do the wrong thing (not meeting the objectives and goals)?

Saying no can be a yes

Why do we have meetings at work? It seems that having conversations in real-time in the same room or virtual space should be highly efficient, with no emails, no delays, only progress, and more progress. However, this is not the case. In a given week, you might have attended many meetings and feel extremely busy, but you might still go home at the end of Friday feeling you hardly got anything done! How is this possible? This was my experience a few years ago when I joined a new company. My new role required strategic thinking and building relationships across the organisation. After a few months in the company, my weekly calendar was overloaded with meetings and durations. I wondered how I would deliver and manage expectations with my line manager.

The situation worsened when I was assigned a business process to lead; that was when I decided to act. I questioned why I was invited to attend a meeting for everyone appearing on my calendar. Some of them were important, but for others, I would request that the organisers provide the rationale for my attendance and expectations.

Based on the feedback received on my requests, I concluded that half of the meetings I attended were only for status reasons because of my position in the company. This was a nice finding in some ways, and I started to decline those where the seat mattered more than getting things done. If the reasons for attending or the expectations are not defined upfront, then I do not need to attend.

It took me some time, but I steadily reduced the meeting load to nearly half what it had been, opening up time to think and efficiently contribute to those I attended. I spent more time connecting with others, supporting my direct reports, and preparing focused and efficient meetings as a project lead (planning and more planning).

I am now sure that attending many meetings is not the real problem; the real problem is that many of those are ineffective. There is some logic behind this; if those were effective, the number would be reduced, correct?

CHAPTER 6
CLOSING THE LOOP

In this book, I have related several stories and described daily situations in our professional environment and when working with others. One aspect we all struggle with is the individual's ability to make everything more complicated than it should be.

As discussed earlier, complexity bias drives individuals to prefer complicated solutions and explanations over simple ones. Like any other bias, it is a complex phenomenon deeply rooted in societal structures and individual perceptions. Human biases develop from our ability to think. By not thinking, other living creatures seem to take a more pragmatic approach to their daily activities. I wonder if human lives would improve without this capability—a bit of a waste after thousands of years of evolution.

You probably agree that complexity bias complicates human lives in business processes unnecessarily. The use of long, wordy sentences in our speech, documents, or presentations; jargon; the addition of "nice-to-haves/non-essentials" to documents; inviting many participants to a meeting when fewer would do the job; and the lack of constructive questioning leading to wrong assumptions are some mechanisms humans use in the work environment. These behaviours may seem to act as independent entities with no correlation. However, with a zoom-out lens, one can group them into a principle deeply ingrained in human behaviour: "the principle of self-preservation."

Freud defines self-preservation as the fundamental tendency of humans and nonhuman animals to avoid injury and maximize their chances of survival—an evolutionary solid trait. For humans, the survival instinct that worked for our primitive ancestors does not necessarily work in modern life. In this context, danger does not imply a physical threat to our lives, but our bodies still automatically respond in the same way when an event is perceived as stressful or frightening.

At this point, you may wonder how the many stories I have described in this book and human survival are related.

People benefit from making things complex in the business environment; otherwise, the desire to complicate things would not be so familiar. We do not want our jobs or positions threatened; we wish to maintain a competitive advantage over our colleagues, and we need to feel that we are significant contributors. It seems that mistakes or failures in the work environment would hinder our options for survival, and we feel threatened when this occurs.

Reflecting on the many strategies humans adopt in the work environment that result in complexity, I think this could come down to "fear." The fear of not being able to communicate adequately, the fear of leaving important information out, or the fear of missing information or hurting people's feelings when keeping them out of meetings can make humans do the exact opposite: adding unnecessary text to documents or slides or inviting more people than required, for example. The constant fear of failing, making errors, or underperforming runs on autopilot in the background and drives many of our decisions. This becomes more prominent in colleagues with low self-confidence levels, making me think that a correlation exists between both: the higher the number of unnecessary words you use, the lower your self-confidence. Self-awareness helps us identify our true motivations when taking specific actions or decisions.

There is another exciting aspect of complexity that I would like to highlight. Some individuals hide behind it as a shield for their insecurities and fears. It is often the case that a colleague in trouble due to poor performance, for example, will find a way of sucking you into layers of confusion and chaos. Ultimately, you might even feel sorry for them and blame everything or everybody else for their problems like they do.

Unsurprisingly, companies developed ways of doing things and established a culture that most would obey. Whether someone has been at a company for years or is interviewing, it is essential to fit in with its corporate culture. The challenge here is that in an environment full of complexity and confusion, many may hide behind "this culture" when facing challenges and difficulties. *"This is how we do things here; things take months or even years!"* a leader once told me. This remark, which I often hear, makes my stomach turn, particularly from leaders. I always wonder, *"Are you saying what happens in this company has nothing to do with you?"* I never dared to ask this question for obvious reasons. It will not surprise you that those making such comments would invite 15+ people to a meeting scheduled to simplify a process, for example. The good news is that many take accountabilities for what happens around them, leading by example and influencing their surroundings, regardless of their positions—a very inspiring way to be!

All these behaviours are simply self-preservation, survival, and a reflection of who we are. Our brain may have gone through millions of years of evolution, but some sections are very primitive and animalistic: the reptilian brain. This part is constantly scanning the environment for threats, which is the root cause of stress and anxiety. The reptilian brain craves comfort and familiarity and fears change and new experiences because they could potentially risk our lives. Our creativity and intuition are hindered when we are in survival mode, and assumptions and beliefs take a primary role. As a result, we may miss opportunities that are potentially beneficial to us. In some ways, we become slaves to our primal instincts. For example, you could miss a great job opportunity for fear of change, even though your current job is tedious, and you find your boss obnoxious.

However, not all is lost. Through years of evolution, the human brain has developed the remarkable ability to reason and the capacity to observe our thoughts, feelings, and emotions. We can step back and view them objectively from a distance. By stepping outside, ourselves, we can leave behind the drama that often consumes our minds.

In doing so, a whole new world of possibilities unfolds before us. If we take the time to pay attention, we will discover a realm brimming with immense and wonderful opportunities. It is a world waiting to be explored, where every moment holds the potential for growth and transformation. So, dare to venture beyond the confines of your mind, and you will be amazed at what awaits you.

Printed in Great Britain
by Amazon

46030269R00056